A *Literature Kit*™ FOR

The Whipping Boy

By Sid Fleischman

Written by Mary-Helen Goyetche

GRADES 5 - 6

Classroom Complete Press
P.O. Box 19729
San Diego, CA 92159
Tel: 1-800-663-3609 | Fax: 1-800-663-3608
Email: service@classroomcompletepress.com

www.classroomcompletepress.com

ISBN-13: 978-1-55319-340-1
ISBN-10: 1-55319-340-7

© 2007

Permission to Reproduce

Permission is granted to the individual teacher who purchases one copy of this book to reproduce the student activity material for use in his or her classroom only. Reproduction of these materials for colleagues, an entire school or school system, or for commercial sale is strictly prohibited. No part of this publication may be transmitted in any form or by any means, electronic, mechanical, recording or otherwise without the prior written permission of the publisher. We acknowledge the financial support of the Government of Canada through the Book Publishing Industry Development Program (BPIDP) for our publishing activities. Printed in Canada. All rights reserved.

Critical Thinking Skills

The Whipping Boy

Skills For Critical Thinking	Chapter Questions 1-2	3-4	5-6	7-8	9-10	11-12	13-14	15-16	17-18	19-20	Writing Tasks	Graphic Organizers
LEVEL 1 Knowledge • Identify Story Elements • Recall Details • Match • Sequence	✓ ✓ ✓ ✓	✓ ✓	✓	✓ ✓ ✓	✓ ✓	✓ ✓	✓ ✓ ✓	✓ ✓ ✓	✓ ✓ ✓ ✓		✓	✓ ✓ ✓
LEVEL 2 Comprehension • Compare & Contrast • Summarize • State Main Idea • Describe • Classify	✓ ✓ ✓			✓ ✓ ✓		✓ ✓ ✓	✓ ✓ ✓ ✓	✓ ✓	✓		✓ ✓ ✓	✓ ✓ ✓ ✓ ✓
LEVEL 3 Application • Plan • Interview • Make Inferences	✓ ✓	✓ ✓	✓ ✓	✓ ✓	✓ ✓	 ✓	✓	✓ ✓	✓ ✓ ✓	✓	✓ ✓	✓
LEVEL 4 Analysis • Draw Conclusions • Identify Supporting Evidence • Infer Character Motivations • Identify Cause & Effect	✓ ✓ ✓	✓ ✓ ✓	✓ ✓ ✓ ✓	✓ ✓ ✓	✓ ✓ ✓	✓ ✓	✓	✓ ✓ ✓ ✓	✓ ✓ ✓	✓		✓ ✓ ✓ ✓
LEVEL 5 Synthesis • Predict • Design (i.e., An Invitation) • Create • Imagine Alternatives	✓	✓	✓ ✓	✓	✓ ✓	✓ ✓	✓ ✓	✓ ✓ ✓	✓	✓	 ✓ ✓	 ✓
LEVEL 6 Evaluation • State & Defend An Opinion • Make Judgements	✓ ✓	✓ ✓	✓ ✓	✓ ✓	✓ ✓	✓ ✓	✓ ✓	✓ ✓	✓ ✓	✓ ✓	✓	

Based on Bloom's Taxonomy

Contents

TEACHER GUIDE
- Assessment Rubric 4
- How Is Our **Literature Kit**™ Organized? 5
- Graphic Organizers 6
- Bloom's Taxonomy for Reading Comprehension 7
- Teaching Strategies 7
- Summary of the Story 8
- Vocabulary 9

STUDENT HANDOUTS
- Spotlight on Sid Fleischman 10
- Chapter Questions
    - *Chapters 1 – 2* 11
    - *Chapters 3 – 4* 14
    - *Chapters 5 – 6* 17
    - *Chapters 7 – 8* 20
    - *Chapter 9 – 10* 23
    - *Chapters 11 – 12* 26
    - *Chapters 13 – 14* 29
    - *Chapters 15 – 16* 32
    - *Chapters 17 – 18* 35
    - *Chapters 19 – 20* 38
- Writing Tasks 41
- Word Search 44
- Comprehension Quiz 45

EASY MARKING™ ANSWER KEY 47

GRAPHIC ORGANIZERS 53

FREE! 6 Bonus Activities!

3 EASY STEPS to receive your 6 Bonus Activities!
- Go to our sister company's website:
  www.classroomcompletepress.com\bonus
- Click on item CC2508 – The Whipping Boy
- Enter pass code CC2508D

Assessment Rubric

The Whipping Boy

Student's Name: _____ Assignment: _____ Level: _____

	Level 1	Level 2	Level 3	Level 4
Comprehension of the Novel	Demonstrates a limited understanding of the novel.	Demonstrates a basic understanding of the novel	Demonstrates a good understanding of the novel	Demonstrates a thorough understanding of the novel
Content	Information incomplete; key details missing	Some information complete; details missing	All required information complete; key details contain some description	All required information complete; enough description for clarity
Style	Little variety in word choice; language vague and imprecise	Some variety in word choice; language somewhat vague and imprecise	Good variety in word choice; language precise and quite descriptive	Writer's voice is apparent throughout. Excellent choice of words; precise language.
Conventions	Errors seriously interfere with the writer's purpose	Repeated errors in mechanics and usage	Some errors in convention	Few errors in convention

STRENGTHS:

WEAKNESSES:

NEXT STEPS:

Before You Teach

Teacher Guide

Our resource has been created for ease of use by both **TEACHERS** and **STUDENTS** alike.

Introduction

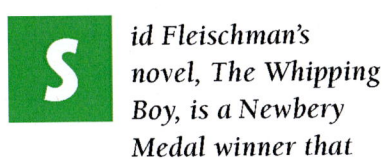

Sid Fleischman's novel, The Whipping Boy, is a Newbery Medal winner that is set in the medieval times. It is the outrageous adventure of a young mischievous prince (nicknamed Prince Brat) and his whipping boy, Jemmy – two boys who could not be more different from each other. One night, the Prince decides to run away and takes Jemmy with him. The boys are faced with more than they bargained for when they run into two outlaws…. Written in a lively and humorous way, this novel is superb read aloud, and is excellent as part of a medieval unit of study.

How Is Our Literature Kit™ Organized?

STUDENT HANDOUTS

Chapter Activities (in the form of reproducible worksheets) make up the majority of this resource. For each chapter or group of chapters there are BEFORE YOU READ activities and AFTER YOU READ activities.

- The BEFORE YOU READ activities prepare students for reading by setting a purpose for reading. They stimulate background knowledge and experience, and guide students to make connections between what they know and what they will learn. Important concepts and vocabulary from the chapter(s) are also presented.

- The AFTER YOU READ activities check students' comprehension and extend their learning. Students are asked to give thoughtful consideration of the text through creative and evaluative short-answer questions and journal prompts.

Six **Writing Tasks** and three **Graphic Organizers** are included to further develop students' critical thinking and writing skills, and analysis of the text. (See page 6 for suggestions on using the Graphic Organizers.) The **Assessment Rubric** (page 4) is a useful tool for evaluating students' responses to the Writing Tasks and Graphic Organizers.

PICTURE CUES

This resource contains three main types of pages, each with a different purpose and use. A **Picture Cue** at the top of each page shows, at a glance, what the page is for.

Teacher Guide
- Information and tools for the teacher

Student Handout
- Reproducible worksheets and activities

Easy Marking™ Answer Key
- Answers for student activities

EASY MARKING™ ANSWER KEY

Marking students' worksheets is fast and easy with this **Answer Key**. Answers are listed in columns – just line up the column with its corresponding worksheet, as shown, and see how every question matches up with its answer!

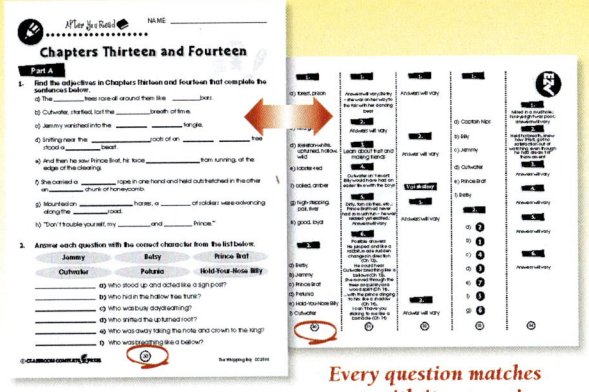

Every question matches up with its answer!

Before You Teach

1, 2, 3
Graphic Organizers

The three **Graphic Organizers** included in our **Literature Kit™** are especially suited to a study of **The Whipping Boy**. Below are suggestions for using each organizer in your classroom, or they may be adapted to suit the individual needs of your students. The organizers can be used on a projection system or interactive whiteboard in teacher-led activities, and/or photocopied for use as student worksheets.
To evaluate students' responses to any of the organizers, you may wish to use the **Assessment Rubric** (on page 4).

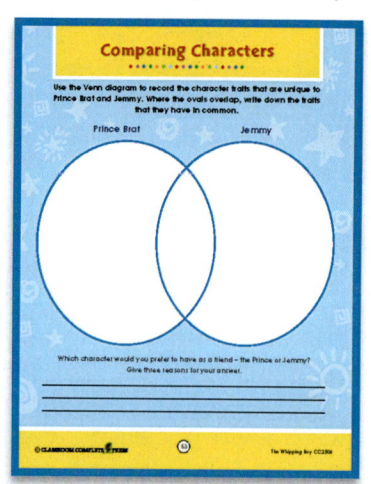

COMPARING CHARACTERS

For this activity students are asked to complete a Venn diagram comparing both boys in the story. Quickly they will realize that the boys do not have many things in common, but they manage to develop a friendship. This is a good exercise for recalling characteristics and traits of the two main characters. The students are also asked for a concluding answer as to which character they would choose to have as a friend. This organizer can also be use to compare themselves with one of the boys, compare the two outlaws, or compare this prince with a prince from another story. **Found on Page 53.**

BEFORE AND AFTER

This graphic organizer is a useful tool to help students identify how Prince Brat changes as a person/character over the course of the novel (a period of just twenty-four hours). Students are asked to describe his character at the beginning of the novel (what kind of person was he?), and then analyze how he had grown and matured by the end of the book. This organizer gives students the opportunity to see that significant (and even lasting) change is possible as a result of the experiences one has in their life. **Found on Page 54.**

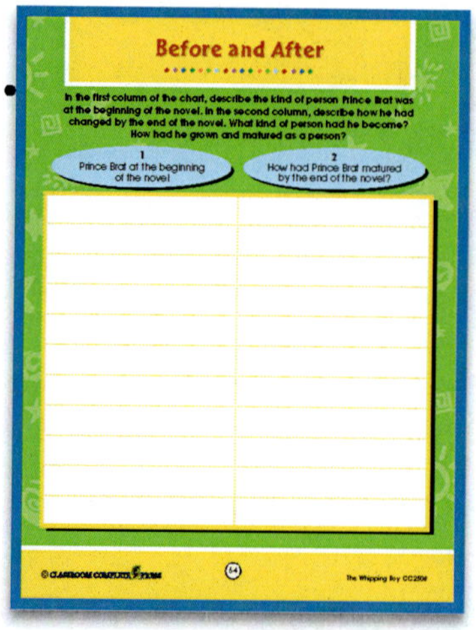

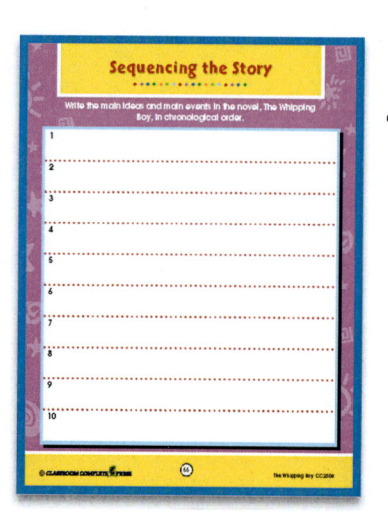

SEQUENCING THE STORY

For this activity students are to write a few sentences stating the main event and main ideas in the story in a chronological order. This organizer can be completed individually, in small groups, or as a class. Each student can write down their own responses, and then in pairs, share their work and make necessary changes. Students can check their own work by looking back through the novel for the information. This is a good exercise for recalling the events of the story in the proper order, and it can be used with any novel. Students can also use it to plan their own creative writing piece. **Found on Page 55.**

Before You Teach

Bloom's Taxonomy* for Reading Comprehension

The activities in this resource engage and build the full range of thinking skills that are essential for students' reading comprehension. Based on the six levels of thinking in Bloom's Taxonomy, questions are given that challenge students to not only recall what they have read, but move beyond this to understand the text through higher-order thinking. By using higher-order skills of application, analysis, synthesis and evaluation, students become active readers, drawing more meaning from the text, and applying and extending their learning in more sophisticated ways.

This **Literature Kit™**, therefore, is an effective tool for any Language Arts program. Whether it is used in whole or in part, or adapted to meet individual student needs, this resource provides teachers with the important questions to ask, inspiring students' interest, creativity, and promoting meaningful learning.

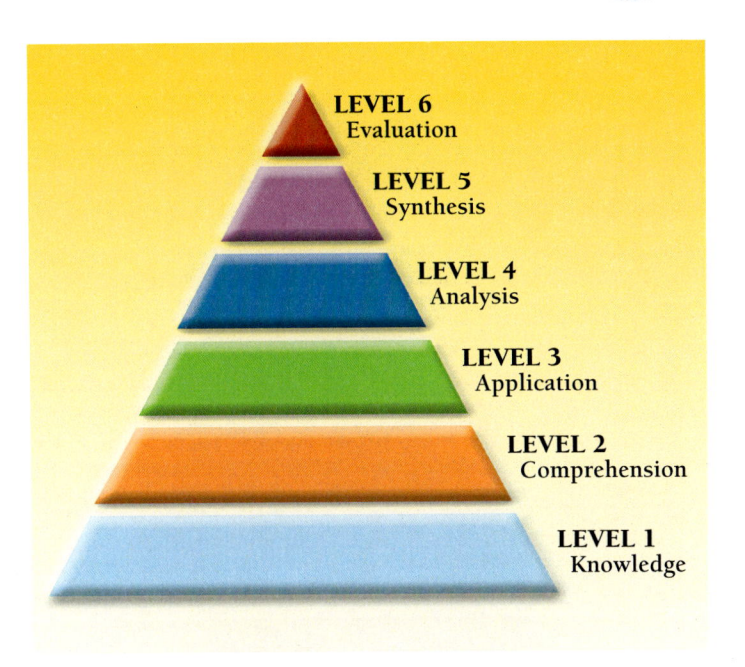

BLOOM'S TAXONOMY: 6 LEVELS OF THINKING

- LEVEL 6 Evaluation
- LEVEL 5 Synthesis
- LEVEL 4 Analysis
- LEVEL 3 Application
- LEVEL 2 Comprehension
- LEVEL 1 Knowledge

Bloom's Taxonomy is a widely used tool by educators for classifying learning objectives, and is based on the work of Benjamin Bloom.

Teaching Strategies — WHOLE-CLASS, SMALL GROUP AND INDEPENDENT STUDY

The Whipping Boy is a novel that may be approached in several ways. Most obvious is as a traditional, whole-class read-aloud in which the teacher reads the book out loud to the entire class, stopping after one or more chapters for the students to answer the chapter questions. As they complete the questions, students reread the chapter(s) on their own. Depending on the interests and needs of your students, you may choose to apply some shared or modeled reading, focusing discussion on the author's skills, choices made in writing, and the elements of the narrative. The BEFORE YOU READ and AFTER YOU READ activities in this **Literature Kit™** provide a basis for such discussions.

To facilitate small group and independent study learning, these activities have been divided into chapter groupings to allow students to work on manageable sections of the novel, and not feel overwhelmed by the activities. Teachers may also choose to use only a selection of the activities in this resource for small group or independent study, assigning tasks that match students' specific needs, and allowing students to work at their own speed. The components of this resource make it flexible and easy to adapt, as not all of the activities need to be completed.

Teachers may wish to have their students keep a daily reading log so that they might record their daily progress and reflections. Journaling prompts have been included at the end of each chapter section to facilitate students' thinking and writing.

Before You Teach

Summary of the Story

AN OUTRAGEOUSLY funny adventure of unlikely friends, murderers, and mistaken identity.

This is the story of the michievous young Prince Horace (nicknamed "Prince Brat" to everyone who knows him) and his whipping boy, Jemmy. Set in the medieval times when extreme social injustices were the order of the day, it was also a time when it was forbidden for a prince to be beaten, whacked, spanked, thrashed or whipped. Jemmy is an orphan boy, plucked from the streets to be the prince's whipping boy – he receives the prince's punishment whenever the boy misbehaves. Unfortunately for Jemmy, Prince Brat gets his whipping boy whipped more times than he can count! The two boys could not have any less in common with each other, let alone any reason for a friendship.

Things change dramatically for the youngsters when, one night, the prince has a wild idea to run away. The only problem is that he is afraid of the dark. So he decides to take his whipping boy with him. Soon after they leave, they run into two outlaws, Hold-Your-Nose Billy and Cutwater, criminals with a record of thievery and murder! The ruffians recognize Prince Brat as a member of the royal family and heir to the throne, and seeing a grand opportunity for themselves, take the boys as hostages. Three breathtaking and nerve-racking adventures follow for the boys, involving mistaken identity.

As the story unfolds, a ransom note is written to the king in which the outlaws demand an entire cartload of gold in exchange for the boys. This rolicking story takes place, from beginning to end, in just twenty-four hours, and finally ends after the boys' last adventure under the city in the sewers.

In keeping with the overall tone of the novel, the story ends with Prince Brat and Jemmy returning safely to the castle. The king forgives the boys ("One more thing," he says. "If you boys decide to run away again, take me with you!"), the whipping boy is no longer whipped, and the two boys remain friends.

Suggestions for Further Reading

OTHER BOOKS BY SID FLEISCHMAN

Bandit's Moon © 1998
Chancy and the Grand Rascal © 1997
The Ghost on Saturday Night © 1997
Mr. Mysterious & Company © 1997
The Abracadabra Kid © 1996
Here Comes McBroom! © 1992
Jim Ugly © 1992
McBroom's Wonderful One-Acre Farm © 1992
The Midnight Horse © 1990
The Scarebird © 1987

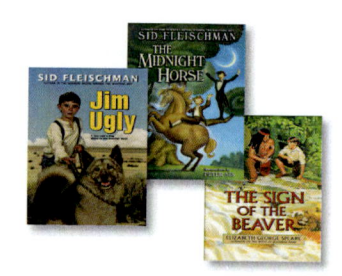

OTHER RECOMMENDED RESOURCES
Elizabeth George Speare, *The Sign of the Beaver* ©1983
Katherine Paterson, *The Great Gilly Hopkins* ©1978
Katherine Paterson, *Bridge to Terabithia* © 1977
Anna Sewell, *Black Beauty* © 1877

Vocabulary

CHAPTERS 1 AND 2
• cackle • contrite • cuff • defiantly • exasperation • furious • gloat • scalped • breeches • contrary • cross • ferrets • obliged • smirking • spectacles • spite

CHAPTERS 3 AND 4
• astonishment • bolt • dreadful • gallows • gory-eyed • mischief • protected • scragged • cleaver • cutthroat • edged • fiercest • halter • insolent • stray

CHAPTERS 5 AND 6
• awe • cold • exploits • rogus • ruffian • thimbleful • thunderclap • bleated • heft • lawks • thatched • trifle • wisps

CHAPTERS 7 AND 8
• afoot • amiss • arrogant • curs • flummox • gnat • witless • bangers • flourish • mite • muxxed • sacred • scoundrels • seize • sullenly

CHAPTER 9 AND 10
• chaw • contemplated • fend • flog • grub • oafs • obedient • ration • scoffed • varmints • indifference • leery • mite • pretense • simpleton • treason

CHAPTERS 11 AND 12
• confounded • errands • generosity • imposter • mulishness • parley • dunce • ruffian • truss

CHAPTERS 13 AND 14
• blabber-tongued • bristled • bustled • confounded • merest • thoroughbred • barnacle • gnat • grimy • resentment • snoutful

CHAPTERS 15 AND 16
• embarkment • mired • mudlarking • stave • ventured • ante • flummox • girded • scheme • scurvy • surge

CHAPTERS 17 AND 18
• hazard • incident • rein • scruffy • spectacles • treasonous • gorged • immense • turf • dodged • hubbub

CHAPTERS 19 AND 20
• brewery • derelict • elation • haughtiness • inaudible • manacle • receded • retreat • convict • notorious • speck • ushered • verge

Spotlight On...

Sid Fleischman

Sid Fleischman was born in Brooklyn, New York. His parents moved to San Diego, California where Sid grew up.

His childhood was during the Great Depression and when he was a child, he dreamt of becoming a magician. When he finished high school, he played vaudeville (a theatre much like a modern day variety show).

Sid spent some time with the U.S. Naval Reserve and after the war he went to college. After college, he worked as a reporter for the San Diego Daily Journal.

Sid got married and had children. He wrote a book for his children and that is how Sid Fleischman became a children's writer. More than 60 books later, he is writing more children's books – all funny and witty.

One of his children, Paul Fleischman, is also a children's writer. He wrote Joyful Noise. Both father and son are the only father/son team to have both received the Newbery Medal.

Today Sid lives in Santa Monica, California. You can write to him by sending your letter to his publisher.

Did You Know?

Sid Fleischman and illustrator, Peter Sis, have collaborated on other books:
- The Ghost In The Noonday Sun (1965)
- The Scarebird (1987)
- The Midnight Horse (1990)
- The 13th Floor: A Ghost Story (1995)

NAME: _____

Before You Read

Chapters One and Two

Answer the questions in complete sentences.

1. What do you know about the **Middle Ages**? What was daily life like for common people? What was it like for royalty? Briefly describe some of the major **differences** between daily life in this period compared to modern times.
   _____
   _____

2. Look carefully at the illustration on the front cover of the novel, The Whipping Boy. What is it a picture of? Based on this illustration, what do you think the novel will be about?
   _____
   _____

Vocabulary

Write each word beside its definition. Then use each word in a sentence that shows its meaning.

cackle   contrary   defiant   exasperate   furious   smirk

1. _____ To resist or show unwillingness to follow the opposition
   _____

2. _____ To aggravate
   _____

3. _____ Extreme anger
   _____

4. _____ To laugh in a harsh and sharp manner
   _____

5. _____ One of a pair of opposites
   _____

6. _____ To smile in a smug manner
   _____

After You Read

NAME: _____

Chapters One and Two

Part A

1. Circle **T** if the statement is **TRUE** or **F** if it is **FALSE**.

   T   F   **a)** Jemmy and Prince Brat were the best of friends.

   T   F   **b)** Jemmy was also known as the whipping boy.

   T   F   **c)** No one ever called the Prince, "Prince Brat" in front of him.

   T   F   **d)** Prince Brat had received too many spankings in his lifetime so now he had a whipping boy.

   T   F   **e)** The Prince thought that Jemmy wasn't howling from each beating to spite him.

   T   F   **f)** After a year, Jemmy left the Prince and ran away.

2. **Number the events from 1 to 6 in the order they occurred in the chapters.**

   _____ **a)** The whipping boy was given twenty whacks.

   _____ **b)** Prince Brat tied the wigs of the King's guests to their chairs and ruined the feast.

   _____ **c)** Jemmy learned to read, to write, and to do sums.

   _____ **d)** A common boy was kept at the castle to receive the Prince's punishment.

   _____ **e)** The Prince was being tutored by Master Peckwit.

   _____ **f)** The Prince was upset with Jemmy for being so quiet.

NAME: _____

After You Read

Chapters One and Two

Part B

Answer the questions in complete sentences.

1. Describe the character of **Prince Brat**. What kind of person is he? Give evidence from the chapters to support your answer.
   _____
   _____

2. Describe the character of **Jemmy**. What kind of person is he? Give evidence from the chapters to support your answer.
   _____
   _____

3. Jemmy seems to accept his role of whipping boy without complaining. Why do you think this is so? Does he have any other options?
   _____
   _____

4. Is Prince Brat fearful that he too will get a whacking? Give reasons for your answer.
   _____
   _____

5. This novel is set during the Middle Ages. How important do you think it was for young people to learn to read, write and do sums in those times?
   _____
   _____

Journal Activity

Using the information from the first two chapters, write about the role of the whipping boy. Who decides who will be a whipping boy? How is a whipping boy found? Why were royal children not punished for their own misbehavior? What would it be like to be someone's whipping boy? How would it feel to be a whipping boy? Do you think the whipping boy was a real role in historical times, or is it just something the author made up to create an interesting story?

© CLASSROOM COMPLETE PRESS

The Whipping Boy CC2508

Before You Read

NAME: _____

Chapters Three and Four

Answer the questions in complete sentences.

1. What do you think will happen to Jemmy, the whipping boy? Do you think reading, writing and doing sums will be beneficial to him? Why or why not?
   _____
   _____

2. Have you ever thought of running away from home? What were your reasons for wanting to leave? What options, besides running away, do young people have when they disagree with their parents?
   _____
   _____

Vocabulary

Write each word next to its synonyms. (Remember: synonyms are different words that have the same or similar meanings). Use a dictionary to help you.

astonishment   bolted   dreadful   fierce

halter   insolent   mischief   strayed

1. Left, departed, fled _____
2. Awful, terrible, unspeakable _____
3. Roamed, wandered, rambled _____
4. Restrain, limit _____
5. Devilry, roguery, rascality _____
6. Savage, ferocious _____
7. Audacious, brassy, barefaced _____
8. Amazement, surprise _____

NAME: _____

After You Read

Chapters Three and Four

Part A

1. **Put a check mark next to the answer that is most correct.**

   a) **What did Prince Brat need when he woke up Jemmy?**
      - ◯ A   A manservant.
      - ◯ B   A womanservant.
      - ◯ C   A butler.

   b) **What was wrong with the Prince?**
      - ◯ A   He was tired.
      - ◯ B   He was bored.
      - ◯ C   He was dumb.

   c) **Why did Prince Brat want to do it at that moment?**
      - ◯ A   It was night time.
      - ◯ B   It was morning.
      - ◯ C   It was right before supper.

   d) **What will the King do when he finds them?**
      - ◯ A   Nothing to Jemmy, but he'll hang the Prince.
      - ◯ B   Nothing to the Prince, but he'll hang Jemmy.
      - ◯ C   He'll hang both of them.

   e) **What was the weather like when they left?**
      - ◯ A   Foggy
      - ◯ B   Snowy
      - ◯ C   Sunny

2. **Which answer best describes:**

   a) **How Jemmy felt as they were leaving?**
      - ◯ A   Excited
      - ◯ B   Sad
      - ◯ C   Thoughtful

   b) **How Jemmy responded when the Prince told him about his plan?**
      - ◯ A   He agreed.
      - ◯ B   He protested.
      - ◯ C   He said he'd think about it.

After You Read

NAME: _____

Chapters Three and Four

Part B

Answer the questions in complete sentences.

1. Do you think Prince Brat had a good plan? Why or why not?
   _____
   _____

2. Why is Prince Brat bored?
   _____
   _____

3. What could Prince Brat do to overcome his boredom?
   _____
   _____

4. What dangers might Jemmy and the Prince be faced with by running away in the middle of the night?
   _____
   _____

5. What lies do you think Prince Brat will tell the King if they get caught?
   _____
   _____

6. Authors often use literary devices to make their writing interesting. A **simile** is a literary device that makes a comparison between two different things using the words *like* or *as*. In Chapter Four, Jemmy thinks the second cutthroat has "**a nose like a meat cleaver**". Try to find **three** more similes in chapters One to Four and write them below.
   _____
   _____

Journal Activity

Reread the part of the story where Jemmy and the Prince meet up with the cutthroats, and the cutthroats are actually two knights under the King's command to find both boys. Pretend that you are the author and write the next chapter back at the castle, where the King confronts Jemmy and Prince Brat. What happens next? Be creative. Give an idea other than the King whipping or hanging Jemmy and not punishing Prince Brat.

NAME: _____

Before You Read

Chapters Five and Six

Answer the questions in complete sentences.

1. What do you predict the cutthroats will do with Prince Brat and Jemmy? What are they looking for?
   _____
   _____

2. Do you think the King's men will search for Prince Brat? Will they search for Jemmy?
   _____
   _____

Vocabulary

Complete each sentence with a word from the list.

| awe | bleated | exploit | rogue |
| ruffian | thatched | thunderclap | wisps |

1. We heard a loud, sharp crash of noise and knew it was a _____.
2. An overwhelming feeling of admiration or of wonder is called _____.
3. _____ of something (like hair) can also be called tufts or locks.
4. A house roof made with plant material is a _____ roof.
5. The prince spoke in a whiny, painful voice; he _____.
6. A person who is cruel and brutal is also known as a _____.
7. A deceitful and unreliable scoundrel can also be called a _____.
8. A notable achievement is quite an _____.

After You Read

NAME: _____

Chapters Five and Six

Part A

1. Circle **T** if the statement is TRUE or **F** if it is FALSE.

   T F **a)** Jemmy and the Prince were captured by the King's knights.

   T F **b)** The outlaws had committed murder during their line of duty.

   T F **c)** The outlaws guessed who the boys were by the basket they were carrying.

   T F **d)** Prince Brat wasn't afraid of the two men.

   T F **e)** The men were sure that the prince was worth his weight in silver.

   T F **f)** Instead of letting them go, the men kept the boys, the basket of food and the crown.

   T F **g)** The men ate off the paper plates and plastic cutlery the Prince brought along.

   T F **h)** When the outlaws were busy eating the boys ran away.

1. Who said the following statements?

   | Cutwater | Hold-Your-Nose Billy | Jemmy | Prince Brat |

   _____ **a)** "Didn't I tell you who I was? Bow low, you fools, and be off!"

   _____ **b)** "Stir your legs. Walk! And don't let me catch you on our turf again. Do I make myself clear?"

   _____ **c)** "Me friend's muddle-headed. His paw's nothing but a rat-catcher. But don't he put on airs, though!"

   _____ **d)** "And I'm the Grand Turnip of China!"

NAME: _____

After You Read

Chapters Five and Six

Part B

Answer the questions in complete sentences.

1. What made the outlaws finally decide to keep the boys?
   _____
   _____

2. How do you think the Prince feels for not being respected as the prince?
   _____
   _____

3. Why is Jemmy trying to pass himself off as the Prince rather than leaving the prince be himself? What would motivate someone to do that for someone else?
   _____
   _____

4. Why do you think the King's men are looking for the boys? Explain your answer.
   _____
   _____

5. How do you think the men became outlaws? Do you think anyone grows up actually wanting to be a criminal?
   _____
   _____

6. How do you feel when someone does not respect you for who you are? How do you get others to respect you?
   _____
   _____

7. By paying attention to the vocabulary words used in this novel we can conclude that the story takes place during a specific historical period. What are some words and phrases that show it is set in the medieval times?
   _____
   _____
   _____

Journal Activity

Have you ever lied to get someone out of trouble? Write the situation that brought you to lie and cover up for someone? What happened after you told your lies? Did this help the other person? Did it help you? Explain what happened. Was it the right thing to do? Will you do it again? Was it worth it? Was it honest?

© CLASSROOM COMPLETE PRESS

The Whipping Boy CC2508

Before You Read

NAME: _____

Chapters Seven and Eight

Answer the questions in complete sentences.

1. What do you think will happen now that the outlaws know they have royalty at their disposal? Do you think they will set them free? When and how?
   _____
   _____

2. Have you ever seen a kidnapping on television? In which movie or television show? Was there a happy ending? Did anyone get hurt? How do you get away from situations like that?
   _____
   _____

Vocabulary

1. **Use a dictionary to find the definitions of the words below. Write each word in a sentence that shows the meaning of the word.**

   a) arrogant _____
   b) witless _____
   c) scoundrel _____
   d) flourish _____
   e) sacred _____
   f) amiss _____
   g) seize _____

2. **Choose two words from the list above that are the least familiar to you. Write each word in a sentence that shows the meaning of the word.**
   _____
   _____

NAME: _____

After You Read

Chapters Seven and Eight

Part A

1. **Answer each question with a word from the list.**

   beet root   veal pie   hawk   crown

   tongue   scoundrels   pheasant   gold

   _____ a) What did Jemmy want Prince Brat to hold?

   _____ b) What did the Prince want to eat?

   _____ c) What type of feather did they need?

   _____ d) Who shouldn't the King cross?

   _____ e) What did Billy use for the ink?

   _____ f) What did Cutwater gnaw on?

   _____ g) What did the Prince bring with him that was found by the outlawed men?

   _____ h) What was the King supposed to leave at the safe spot?

2. **Number the events from 1 to 7 in the order they occurred in the chapters.**

   _____ a) The Prince was complaining that he was hungry.

   _____ b) Jemmy started to write the note.

   _____ c) He convinced them to ask for a wagonload rather than his weight in gold.

   _____ d) Cutwater found paper to write a note.

   _____ e) Jemmy signed the letter as the King's obedient son.

   _____ f) Jemmy and the Prince switched identities.

   _____ g) A document needed to be written before anyone could feast.

After You Read

NAME: _____

Chapters Seven and Eight

Part B

Answer the questions in complete sentences.

1. Describe the **tension** you felt as Jemmy was writing the note, the Prince was complaining, and the two outlaws were getting ready for the trade.
   _____
   _____

2. If someone asked you to write a ransom note, what are some of the items you would use to **negotiate** with?
   _____
   _____

3. Why did the boys switch identities?
   _____
   _____

4. What do think about the boys switching identities? Why was it better for them to switch identities than not?
   _____
   _____

5. Why didn't Jemmy just take off and "sell" the Prince?
   _____
   _____

6. How do you think the switch will change the boys' relationship? How differently do you see Jemmy now? Explain your answer.
   _____
   _____

7. How do you predict the King will react when he reads the ransom note?
   _____
   _____

Journal Activity

Jemmy wrote the ransom note for the outlaws. Nobody other than Jemmy knows how to read. Write the ransom note that Jemmy would most probably write to the King. Do you think he would really add lies as : your obedient son?

© CLASSROOM COMPLETE PRESS   The Whipping Boy CC2508

NAME: _____

Before You Read

Chapters Nine and Ten

Answer the questions in complete sentences.

1. Do you think the outlaws will discover that Jemmy and the Prince switched identities? What do you think will happen if and when they discover this information?
   _____
   _____

2. What plan do you think Jemmy has?
   _____
   _____

Vocabulary

1. **Write each word beside its antonyms. (Remember: antonyms are words that have opposite meanings).**

   considerable   indifferent   leery   obedient
   outlaw   poisonous   treason

   a) _____ insignificant, trivial
   b) _____ contrary, obstinate, wayward
   c) _____ legal
   d) _____ non-toxic, edible, healthy
   e) _____ trusting
   f) _____ concerned
   g) _____ loyal, alliance, bond

2. **Choose two words from the list above and one antonym for each word. Then, for each pair of antonyms, write a sentence that includes both words within the same sentence.**

   _____
   _____

After You Read

Chapters Nine and Ten

Part A

1. Put a check mark next to the answer that is most correct.

a) What was Billy's secret medication to get rid of the plague and clear his head?
- A   Onions
- B   Leeks
- C   Garlic

b) According to Prince Brat, bread and herring isn't fit for whom?
- A   Fish
- B   Flies
- C   Frogs

c) What worries did Cutwater have?
- A   He was worried they were going to run out of food.
- B   He was worried they were going to get caught.
- C   He was worried that the Prince had laid a trap in the letter.

d) What did Billy have Jemmy do?
- A   Read the letter as fast as possible
- B   Read the letter word by word
- C   Read the letter backwards, bottoms up

e) What suggestion did Jemmy have on how to get the letter to the King?
- A   Use the postal system
- B   Send it with the birds
- C   Get the whipping boy to deliver it by hand

f) What proof would give the letter credibility?
- A   The signature and the Prince's handwriting
- B   The letter along with the Prince's crown
- C   The outlaw seal of approval

NAME: _____

After You Read

Chapters Nine and Ten

Part B

Answer the questions in complete sentences.

1. How would the story be different if the outlaws knew how to read and write?

2. Why was Jemmy so insistent that Prince Brat be the one to go and deliver the letter? What could have happened to Prince Brat had he left right away?

3. Did Hold-Your-Nose Billy and Cutwater have the right to argue about who was going? How would you have settled the argument? Who would you have sent? Why?

4. How would the King "loosen" the outlaw's tongue? How did Jemmy know that the King favors slow boiling in oil? How painful could that be?

5. There is a lot of violence described and talked about in The Whipping Boy. Is there the same kind of violence in the world today?

Journal Activity

This story is written in the third-person, meaning that it is told from the *point of view* of a narrator. We do not hear the characters' own private thoughts and feelings as they are experienced. How different would the story be if the author had written the story in the first person, from the point of view of either Jemmy or Prince Brat? Rewrite one passage from chapter Nine or Ten using the point of view of one of the main characters. How different are the two passages?

Before You Read

Chapters Eleven and Twelve

Answer the questions in complete sentences.

1. How will Jemmy react to the latest news that Prince Brat doesn't want to deliver the letter?
   _____
   _____

2. Do you believe that Prince Brat has another plan, or he is frightened to go alone without Jemmy? Explain your answer.
   _____
   _____

Vocabulary

1. **Write each word from the list beside its definition. You may use a dictionary to help you.**

   confounded   dunce   errand   imposter
   parley   ruffian   truss

   a) _____ A person who is slow witted

   b) _____ To put to shame

   c) _____ A metal band around beams used for additional support

   d) _____ A short trip taken to attend to business

   e) _____ A bully; a cruel and mean person

   f) _____ To discuss terms with an enemy

   g) _____ Someone who takes the identity of another person to be deceiving

2. **Choose two words from the list above that are the least familiar to you. Write each word in a sentence that shows the meaning of the word.**
   _____
   _____

NAME: _____

After You Read

Chapters Eleven and Twelve

Part A

1. Circle T if the statement is TRUE or F if it is FALSE.

T F   **a)** Prince Brat took off very quickly after saying he was only farcing.

T F   **b)** The outlaws thought Prince Brat was being greedy.

T F   **c)** Jemmy wanted to talk to Prince Brat alone so that he could talk some sense into him.

T F   **d)** Jemmy was ready to return to the castle and he wanted Prince Brat to go back.

T F   **e)** Prince Brat wasn't ready to go back to the castle; he was the one who wanted to run away.

T F   **f)** Jemmy disappeared under the straw.

T F   **g)** Jemmy is afraid what will happen if the King finds out he wrote the note.

T F   **h)** The boys were planning to move to another city.

2. Who said the following statements?

| Cutwater | Hold-Your-Nose Billy | Jemmy | Prince Brat |

_____ **a)** "It would please me to shake the teeth out of your confounded face!"

_____ **b)** "I'll whip the mulishness out of him!"

_____ **c)** "I'll do what I choose. And I choose not to run your errands."

_____ **d)** "Prince Blockhead! You should wear your crown to fend off woodpeckers."

After You Read

NAME: _____

Chapters Eleven and Twelve

Part B

Answer the questions in complete sentences.

1. How much time do you think has passed from the beginning of Chapter One to the end of Twelve?
   _____
   _____

2. How do you predict the kidnapping will end?
   _____
   _____

3. Why would Billy and Cutwater think Prince Brat wanted a share of the loot?
   _____
   _____

4. What would your plan be if you were one of the characters? Explain your answer.
   _____
   _____

5. Do you think things will get better or worse for Prince Brat? Will they get better or worse for Jemmy? Explain your answers.
   _____
   _____

6. Do you think Hold-Your-Nose Bill and Cutwater will hurt the boys? How old do you think the boys are?
   _____
   _____

Journal Activity

The prince gobbled down an apple tart from the wicker basket. What is your favorite recipe using apples? Write it down, including the list of ingredients, the steps to make it, how long to bake or cook it (if it needs to be cooked), and how many servings the recipe is for. Exchange recipes with your classmates and have an apple day where different recipes can be tried out.

NAME: _____

Before You Read

Chapters Thirteen and Fourteen

Answer the questions in complete sentences.

1. Do you think that the boys will be rescued? Will the King believe the note? Explain your answers.
   _____
   _____

2. The boys are going to a place they have never been to before; yet they never mentioned they were using a map. Will they get lost? Have you or someone you know ever gotten lost? Briefly describe what happened.
   _____
   _____

Vocabulary

Write each word next to its synonyms. (Remember: synonyms are different words that have the same or similar meanings).

| blabber-tongued | bristled | confounded | grimy |
| mere | pondered | resentment | thoroughbred |

1. pedigree, pureblooded   _____
2. bare, simple, plain   _____
3. grubby, grungy   _____
4. befuddled, confused   _____
5. bitterness, rancor, gall   _____
6. squealer, big-mouthed   _____
7. muse, reflect   _____
8. abounded, overflowed   _____

After You Read

NAME: _____

Chapters Thirteen and Fourteen

Part A

1. **Find the adjectives in Chapters Thirteen and Fourteen that complete the sentences below.**

   a) The _____ trees rose all around them like _____ bars.

   b) Cutwater, startled, lost the _____ breath of time.

   c) Jemmy vanished into the _____ _____ tangle.

   d) Sniffing near the _____ roots of an _____ _____ tree stood a _____ beast.

   e) And then he saw Prince Brat, his face _____ from running, at the edge of the clearing.

   f) She carried a _____ rope in one hand and held outstretched in the other an _____ chunk of honeycomb.

   g) Mounted on _____ horses, a _____ of soldiers were advancing along the _____ road.

   h) "Don't trouble yourself, my _____ and _____ Prince."

2. **Answer each question with the correct character from the list below.**

   Jemmy   **Betsy**   **Prince Brat**
   Cutwater   **Petunia**   **Hold-Your-Nose Billy**

   _____ a) Who stood up and acted like a sign post?
   _____ b) Who hid in the hallow tree trunk?
   _____ c) Who was busy daydreaming?
   _____ d) Who sniffed the upturned root?
   _____ e) Who was away taking the note and crown to the King?
   _____ f) Who was breathing like a bellow?

NAME: _____

After You Read

Chapters Thirteen and Fourteen

Part B

Answer the questions in complete sentences.

1. Who is the girl that we meet in Chapter Fourteen? What was she doing in the forest?
   _____
   _____

2. Why do people perform at fairs? Does a person need a special talent to perform? What are some of the similarities and differences between medieval fairs and modern-day fairs?
   _____
   _____

3. What important lesson did Prince Brat learn in these chapters?
   _____
   _____

4. Was it a good idea to leave Cutwater to watch the boys? Why or not?
   _____
   _____

5. Describe what Jemmy and Prince Brat would have looked like at the end of Chapter Fourteen. Why did Prince Brat say that this was the best time he had ever had?
   _____
   _____

6. The author uses lots of interesting similes in these chapters. (A **simile** is a comparison between two different things using the words like or as.) In Chapter Thirteen the author writes, "**Brambles, reaching out like cat's claws, tore at their fine garments**". Try to find **five** more similes in Chapters Thirteen and Fourteen and write them below.
   _____
   _____

Journal Activity

Children and adults alike love country fairs, from the exhibits, to the games, food and entertainment. Create a poster to announce an upcoming local fair. Include specific information such as the date, the times and the location. What attractions will be there? Will any local celebrities be there? Make sure your poster is appealing. Good advertising is the key to a successful event!

Before You Read

Chapters Fifteen and Sixteen

Answer the questions in complete sentences.

1. Do you think Prince Brat is almost ready to go home? What do you think Jemmy wants at this point in the story?
   _____
   _____

2. What do you predict will happen when Hold-Your-Nose Billy finds out that Cutwater lost both boys?
   _____
   _____

Vocabulary

1. **Use a dictionary to find the definitions of the words below.**

   a) mired _____

   b) girded _____

   c) scurvy _____

   d) surge _____

   e) flummox _____

   f) ante _____

   g) scheme _____

   h) ventured _____

2. **Choose two words from the list above that are the least familiar to you. Write each word in a sentence that shows the meaning of the word.**
   _____
   _____

NAME: _____

After You Read

Chapters Fifteen and Sixteen

Part A

1. **Who said each of the following?**

   Jemmy   Betsy   Captain Nips   Prince Brat   Cutwater   Hold-Your-Nose Billy

   _____ a) "Don't mind if I do. I'm late for the fair as it is."

   _____ b) "Swimmed the river! Faw! He'd need scales and fins."

   _____ c) "Lay down your whip. Don't you have an ounce of sense between you?"

   _____ d) "Got one! The whipping boy, it is! Where's your master, eh?"

   _____ e) "Of course I can! I don't need flocks of servants to fetch and carry for me."

   _____ f) "Ruffian! What are you doing to that poor boy?"

2. **Number the events from 1 to 7 in the order they occurred in the chapters.**

   _____ a) Jemmy told Prince Brat he could leave at any time, and then Jemmy started to collect firewood.

   _____ b) The soldiers passed by as Jemmy and Prince Brat hid.

   _____ c) The boys hid between the potatoes just before the outlaws returned.

   _____ d) Prince Brat helped collect wood, and the boys helped Captain Harry Nips because his coach was mired in a mudhole.

   _____ e) Betsy yelled at the ruffians to stop hurting the boy and set Petunia after them.

   _____ f) Billy and Cutwater discovered the boys, and Billy whipped the whipping boy – Prince Brat.

   _____ g) Jemmy yelled at the prince to bawl.

After You Read

NAME: _____

Chapters Fifteen and Sixteen

Part B

1. How did Captain Nips get his cart stuck? What was his excuse? Why did he agree to bring the boys?
   _____
   _____

2. How did Jemmy feel when Prince Brat was being whipped?
   _____
   _____

3. How could Jemmy and Prince Brat have gotten out of this situation?
   _____
   _____

4. Why do you think Betsy came to boy's defense? What else could she have done? What would you have done?
   _____
   _____

5. What kind of person does one have to be to whip another person? When is it **justified** to hurt someone else?
   _____
   _____

6. Have you ever been a witness to bullying? What happened? Who bullied who? How did that make you feel? What did you do to stop it?
   _____
   _____

Journal Activity

Captain Harry Nips didn't intervene when Hold-Your-Nose Billy was whipping Prince Brat. Rewrite this passage and make Captain Harry Nips the hero. How could an old man with poor eyesight save a boy from an outlaw with a whip? Be creative and turn Captain Nips into the hero!

NAME: _____

Before You Read

Chapters Seventeen and Eighteen

Answer the questions in complete sentences.

1. This is the second time Betsy arrived at the right place at the right time. Do you think she will stay with the boys? Why or why not?
   _____
   _____

2. What do you think will happen with Jemmy and Prince Brat now? How will their friendship unfold? Will they go back to the castle, together?
   _____
   _____

Vocabulary

Complete each sentence with a word from the list.

| dodged | hazard | hubbub | immense |
| incident | scruffy | spectacles | turf |

1. When you have trouble reading, you might need _____.

2. It was a frightening _____ when the cars smashed into each other, head on.

3. Smoking cigarettes is a _____ to your health.

4. The dog's fur was all shaggy and _____.

5. The _____ of the party was so loud, it was almost deafening.

6. The tallest mountain in the world, Mount Everest, is _____.

7. Having returned to the city, Jemmy was glad to be back on familiar _____.

8. As they ran through the fair, the boys _____ acrobats and a man walking stilts.

After You Read

NAME: _____

Chapters Seventeen and Eighteen

Part A

1. **Circle T** if the statement is TRUE or **F** if it is FALSE.

   T F **a)** Hold-Your-Nose Billy ended up in the river.

   T F **b)** Petunia, Betsy, Jemmy, and Prince Brat loaded up the cart with Captain Nips and went to city without any other incident.

   T F **c)** The soldiers stopped the cart and found Prince Brat.

   T F **d)** As he entered the city, Jemmy found a rat.

   T F **e)** Captain Nips offered to feed the boys potatoes and bought fresh warm milk for them.

   T F **f)** There were a lot of people at the fair.

   T F **g)** Jemmy met his old friend Smudge.

   T F **h)** Smudge laughed at Jemmy because Jemmy could read, write and do sums.

   T F **i)** Prince Brat introduced himself to Smudge as the Royal Prince.

   T F **j)** Prince Brat was happy he could finally shake someone's hands.

   T F **k)** Jemmy didn't hate Prince Brat anymore.

   T F **l)** The king offered a reward to anyone who could find Captain Harry Nips.

NAME: _____

After You Read

Chapters Seventeen and Eighteen

Part B

Answer the questions in complete sentences.

1. Do you think Jemmy is in danger now? If he is captured, will the King believe his story?
   _____
   _____

2. How do you think the King will react when he finds out the whole idea was Prince Brat's?
   _____
   _____

3. Where do you think the Queen is? What role would she play if she was in the story?
   _____
   _____

4. Why do you think Jemmy made money selling rats? Would you want to buy sewer rats?
   _____
   _____

5. If you were Smudge, would you be happy to see Jemmy again? Would you want to be friends again? Explain your answers.
   _____
   _____

6. How do you think the boys will get caught? Predict how the story will unfold in the last two chapters.
   _____
   _____

Journal Activity

Should Jemmy decide to stay in the sewers, he will eventually have a craving to read. Think of places Jemmy could get books or other reading materials. Make two lists: one of places from the medieval times, and one of places that can be found today. Compare both lists. What conclusion do you arrive at when you compare both lists?

Before You Read

NAME: _____

Chapters Nineteen and Twenty

Answer the questions in complete sentences.

1. How do you think the novel will end?
   _____
   _____

2. a) What will happen to: Hold-Your-Nose Billy?
   _____
   _____

   b) What will become of Jemmy?
   _____
   _____

   c) Will Prince Brat ever become king?
   _____
   _____

Vocabulary

Write each word beside its synonyms. (Remember: synonyms are different words that have the same or similar meanings).

| altered | convict | derelict | elation |
| manacle | notorious | receded | ushered |

1. inmate, jailbird   _____
2. lead, introduced   _____
3. delinquent, vagrant   _____
4. withdrew, retreated   _____
5. shackle, restraint   _____
6. joyousness, happiness   _____
7. changed, varied   _____
8. infamous   _____

NAME: _____

After You Read

Chapters Nineteen and Twenty

Part A

1. ⓒircle the clues that show that Prince Brat had changed during the last twenty-four hours.

Couldn't stand to hear bellowing	Took the whacks intended for the whipping boy	Helped collect firewood
Twinkle in is eye	Hand felt friendly and trusting	Had never had so much fun
Didn't want to go back to the castle without Jemmy	Gave a playfu wink	Prince Brat laughed

2. Number the events from ❶ to ❽ in the order they occurred in the chapters.

_____ a) Jemmy and Prince Brat ran into the sewer tunnel.

_____ b) Huge sewer rat bit both Hold-Your-Nose Billy and Cutwater.

_____ c) Hold-Your-Nose Billy and Cutwater spotted the boys in the sewer.

_____ d) Down in the inner tunnels of the city, the boys ran into Ol' Johnny Tosher.

_____ e) Billy overheard and realized that he whipped the prince and not the whipping boy.

_____ f) Ol' Johnny Tosher told the two outlaws the right way to go.

_____ g) The boys spotted Hold-Your-Nose Billy and Cutwater.

_____ h) Prince Brat laughed, saying, "They look like they're wearing fur coats."

© CLASSROOM COMPLETE PRESS 39 The Whipping Boy CC2508

After You Read NAME: _____

Chapters Nineteen and Twenty

Part B

Answer the questions in complete sentences.

1. Do you like the way this story ends? Why or why not? Give specific examples.
   _____
   _____

2. If you could ask Jemmy some questions, what would you want to know? Why would you want to know these things?
   _____
   _____

3. Do you prefer the Prince we met at the beginning of the novel or the Prince at the end? Why?
   _____
   _____

4. What type of friend will Prince Brat be now? What type of friend will Jemmy be? Will they be different? If so, how will they be different?
   _____
   _____

5. Where do you see the boys five years **after** the end of the story?
   _____
   _____

6. Where do you see the boys **twenty** years later? How will the economy be? How will the King be, and in what condition will the city be? Give reasons for your ideas.
   _____
   _____

Journal Activity

The author, Sid Fleischman, wrote a note at the end of this novel telling readers that <u>The Whipping Boy</u> is a work of fiction, but that unfortunately some of it is true. For example, some royal families did keep a "whipping boy" who was punished instead of the Prince. What do you think about this? How does this make you feel? Write a letter to a King asking him to stop using whipping boys.

📝 Writing Task #1

Chapters 1 to 3

In the novel, <u>The Whipping Boy</u>, we get a sense of what life could have been like for people and their families in the medieval times.

> For this activity you will create your own **coat of arms**. A coat of arms is a shield or banner, and in the medieval times, many families had their own coat of arms. Every symbol, and their colors, shapes and position on the shield had significant, special meaning. Look for information in books, an encyclopedia, or on the Internet to find out what coats of arms looked like in those days. What symbols were used? What colors were used? What did different symbols and colors mean?

Illustrate your own coat of arms and write a brief presentation to share with your classmates.

📝 Writing Task #2

Chapters 4 to 7

Prince Horace is nicknamed "Prince Brat" for a good reason: he is a real nuisance and a real joker.

Choose your favorite passage from Chapters Four to Seven and rewrite it from the Prince's point of view.

> **Think about:**
> - Will he question himself or his actions?
> - Will he be even meaner than the author, Sid Fleischman, has portrayed him?
> - What are the private, inner thoughts, feelings (and maybe even darker secrets) of this terribly lonely boy?

Writing Task #3

Chapters 8 to 12

In Chapter Eight, Jemmy writes a ransom note to the King. He convinces the outlaws to ask not only for the Prince's weight in gold, but for an entire cartload of gold.

> For this activity you will create **two wanted posters**, one for each of the outlaws. On each poster be sure to include the following:
>
> - an illustration of the outlaw
> - a brief summary warning people why these criminals are dangerous
> - the reward you will offer to the person or people who turn them in

You may make your posters funny, or ones that look like real FBI posters.

Writing Task #4

Chapters 13 to 16

In Chapters Sixteen, Cutwater and Hold-Your-Nose Billy are back! These two tough male outlaws are really making the Prince's run away adventure very difficult.

> Suppose these two tough male outlaws were, in fact, **two little girls**. How different would the story be? Choose a passage from Chapters Thirteen to Sixteen and **rewrite** it so that the outlaws are two little girls.

Have fun changing the dynamic of the story. Would the girls be taken seriously? What would they say and do? How would they speak? Would they want to keep the boys or get rid of them? Include the new dialogue between the four characters.

Writing Task #5

Chapter 17 to 18

Prince Brat, Jemmy, Betsy, Petunia and Captain Nips arrive in the city. The boys fetch some water in the cast-iron pot so that they can build a fire and boil a feast of potatoes. Captain Nips also gives money to the boys so they can get fresh, right-out-of-the-cow, warm milk.

Rewrite this passage as if the five characters were coming into a **modern day city**.

- What changes would there be?
- How would technology change the story?
- What would be different?
- What aspects would stay the same?

Writing Task #6

Chapters 19 to 20

At the end of the book, the King tells the boys that if they ever want to run away again, they should let him know so he can join them.

Write the **story outline** that the author, Sid Fleischman, could use to write another adventure about Prince Horace and Jemmy.

Think about:
- What kinds of dangers will they face?
- Will the two outlaws, Cutwater and Hold-Your-Nose Billy, still be a part of the story?
- Will you introduce new characters such as Grab-Your-Arm Willy or Kick-Off-Your-Shoe Fred?
- What do you foresee for Betsy and Petunia? Will they have gone off to join the circus?

After You Read

NAME: _____

Word Search

Find all of the words in the word search. Words may be horizontal, vertical, or diagonal. A few may even be backwards. Look carefully!

arrogant	fiercest	notorious	specatcles
astonishment	gallows	obedient	thimbleful
cleaver	generosity	parley	thunderclap
contemplated	hubbub	resentment	derelict
convict	merest	ruffian	dreadful
cutthroat	mischief	flummox	errands
defiantly	mulishness	seize	exasperation

d	f	t	d	c	a	s	t	o	n	i	s	h	m	e	n	t	d
r	e	b	h	o	p	e	t	h	m	p	m	o	e	l	z	h	r
e	x	f	r	u	a	m	p	e	c	a	l	i	r	a	m	i	e
s	a	t	i	g	n	r	v	e	r	r	b	o	e	t	u	m	a
e	s	h	i	a	t	d	r	n	g	l	c	e	s	i	l	b	d
n	p	i	j	l	n	a	e	o	a	e	o	l	t	o	i	l	f
t	e	l	k	l	k	t	u	r	g	y	e	q	a	n	s	e	u
m	r	o	p	o	r	c	l	v	c	a	e	t	a	b	h	f	l
e	a	w	e	w	g	h	t	y	u	l	n	r	i	f	n	u	c
n	t	m	i	s	c	h	i	e	f	c	a	t	s	l	e	l	o
t	i	n	e	z	o	l	i	j	u	l	m	p	e	u	s	u	n
s	o	a	v	e	g	y	l	t	n	e	o	e	i	m	s	b	t
p	n	w	a	g	g	i	t	g	m	a	m	i	z	m	n	c	e
e	b	d	o	t	w	h	z	x	n	v	b	g	e	o	o	d	m
c	s	m	n	a	r	i	z	a	a	e	l	h	u	x	t	e	p
t	m	q	b	o	b	m	a	s	i	r	y	b	e	e	o	t	l
a	s	j	a	n	g	l	e	a	f	c	d	o	s	d	r	c	a
c	t	t	s	e	c	r	e	i	f	g	t	r	g	m	i	i	t
l	r	u	s	t	w	o	r	t	u	y	o	h	g	m	o	v	e
e	i	j	l	e	f	k	e	r	r	a	n	d	s	t	u	n	d
s	m	l	m	y	t	i	s	o	r	e	n	e	g	h	s	o	c
r	o	m	c	d	d	e	r	e	l	i	c	t	a	f	n	c	a
h	u	b	b	u	b	e	r	i	n	o	b	e	d	i	e	n	t

© CLASSROOM COMPLETE PRESS

44

The Whipping Boy CC2508

NAME: _____

After You Read

Comprehension Quiz

Answer the questions in complete sentences.

1. Name all the major characters in the novel. Name the minor characters.
   _____
   _____

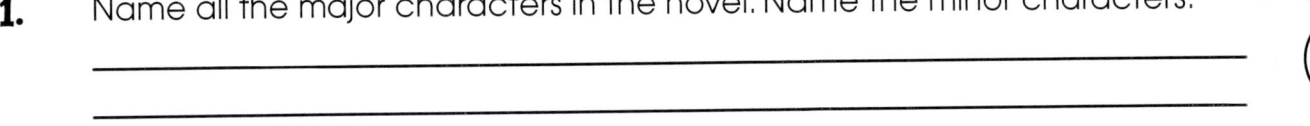

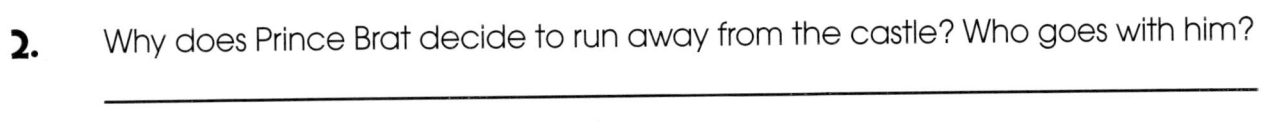

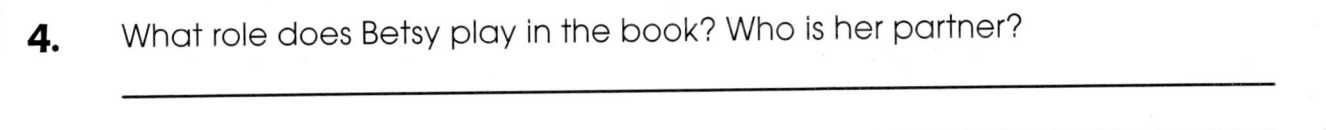

2. Why does Prince Brat decide to run away from the castle? Who goes with him?
   _____
   _____

3. Why is the character, Smudge, important in the story?
   _____
   _____

4. What role does Betsy play in the book? Who is her partner?
   _____
   _____

5. Why is Prince Brat so detestable? What happens when he gets punished?
   _____
   _____

6. What happens to the boys as soon as they get out of the city? Who are they?
   _____
   _____

7. Who wrote the ransom note? Why did the boys switch identities?
   _____
   _____

8. Why is Captain Harry Nips' cart so useful? What is he carrying?
   _____
   _____

9. Who is Petunia? What does Petunia do for the boys?
   _____
   _____

SUBTOTAL: /18

After You Read

Comprehension Quiz

NAME: _____

10. Who was Ol' Johnny Tosher? What was he supposed to do?
    _____
    _____ /2

11. How did Jemmy feel when Prince Brat got his whack from Billy? What did he tell the Prince to do?
    _____
    _____ /2

12. What did Captain Nips give the boys?
    _____
    _____ /2

13. What did the soldiers find when they looked inside the potato cart? What was its name?
    _____
    _____ /2

14. What use did the royal family have with a whipping boy? Where did they get him?
    _____
    _____ /2

15. What did Prince Brat bring in his basket? What things should he have brought instead?
    _____
    _____ /2

16. What was in the black oak chest? What was Cutwater looking for?
    _____
    _____ /2

17. Who turned the boys in to the King? What reaction did the King have?
    _____
    _____ /2

18. What is the setting of the story (time and place)?
    _____
    _____ /2

SUBTOTAL: /18

EZ✓

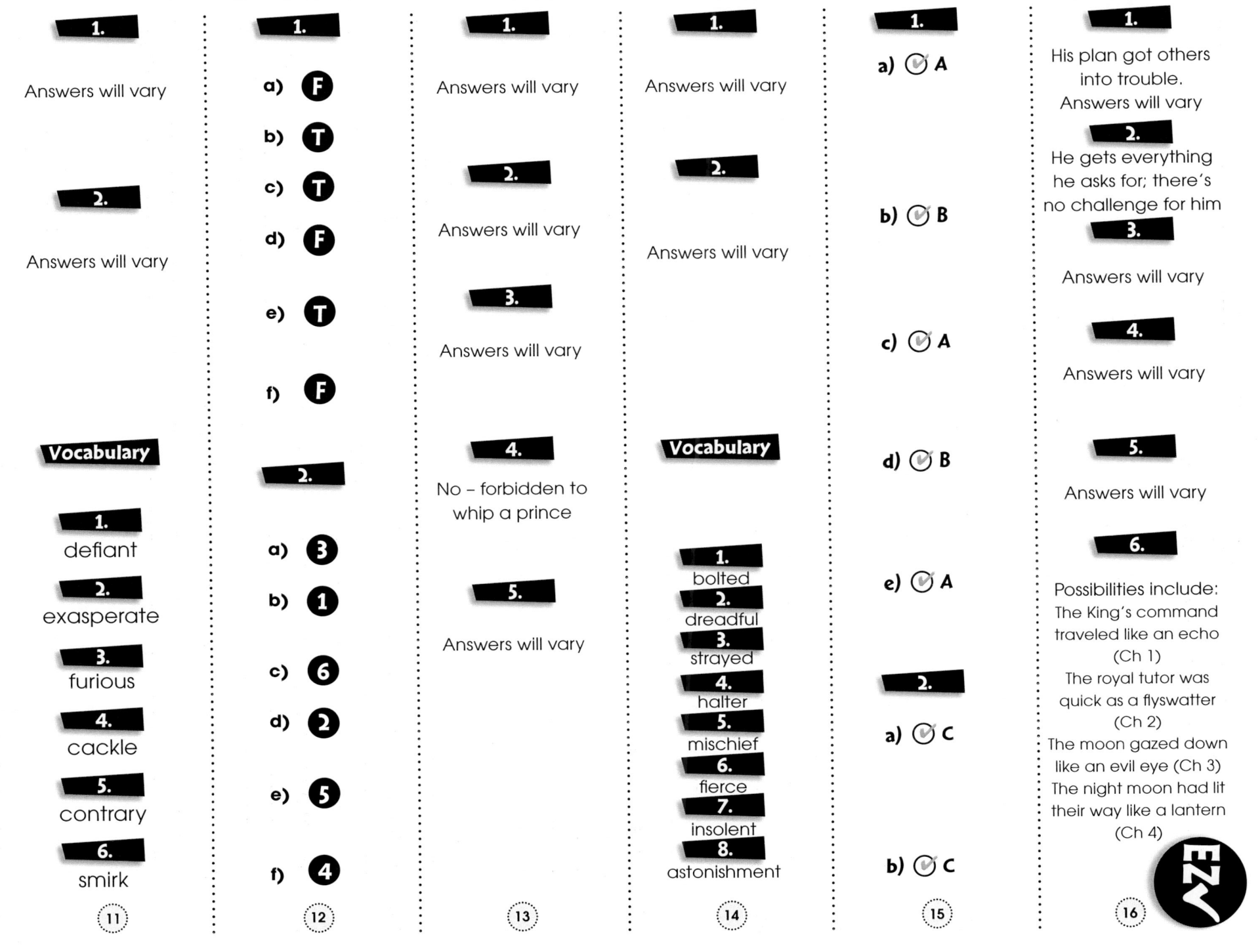

1. His plan got others into trouble. Answers will vary
2. He gets everything he asks for; there's no challenge for him
3. Answers will vary
4. Answers will vary
5. Answers will vary
6. Possibilities include:
The King's command traveled like an echo (Ch 1)
The royal tutor was quick as a flyswatter (Ch 2)
The moon gazed down like an evil eye (Ch 3)
The night moon had lit their way like a lantern (Ch 4)

16

1.
a) A
b) B
c) A
d) B
e) A

2.
a) C
b) C

15

---

1. Answers will vary
2. Answers will vary

Vocabulary
1. bolted
2. dreadful
3. strayed
4. halter
5. mischief
6. fierce
7. insolent
8. astonishment

14

---

1. Answers will vary
2. Answers will vary
3. Answers will vary
4. No – forbidden to whip a prince
5. Answers will vary

13

1.
a) F
b) T
c) T
d) F
e) T
f) F

2.
a) 3
b) 1
c) 6
d) 2
e) 5
f) 4

12

---

1. Answers will vary
2. Answers will vary

Vocabulary
1. defiant
2. exasperate
3. furious
4. cackle
5. contrary
6. smirk

11

© CLASSROOM COMPLETE PRESS

The Whipping Boy CC2508

EZ✓

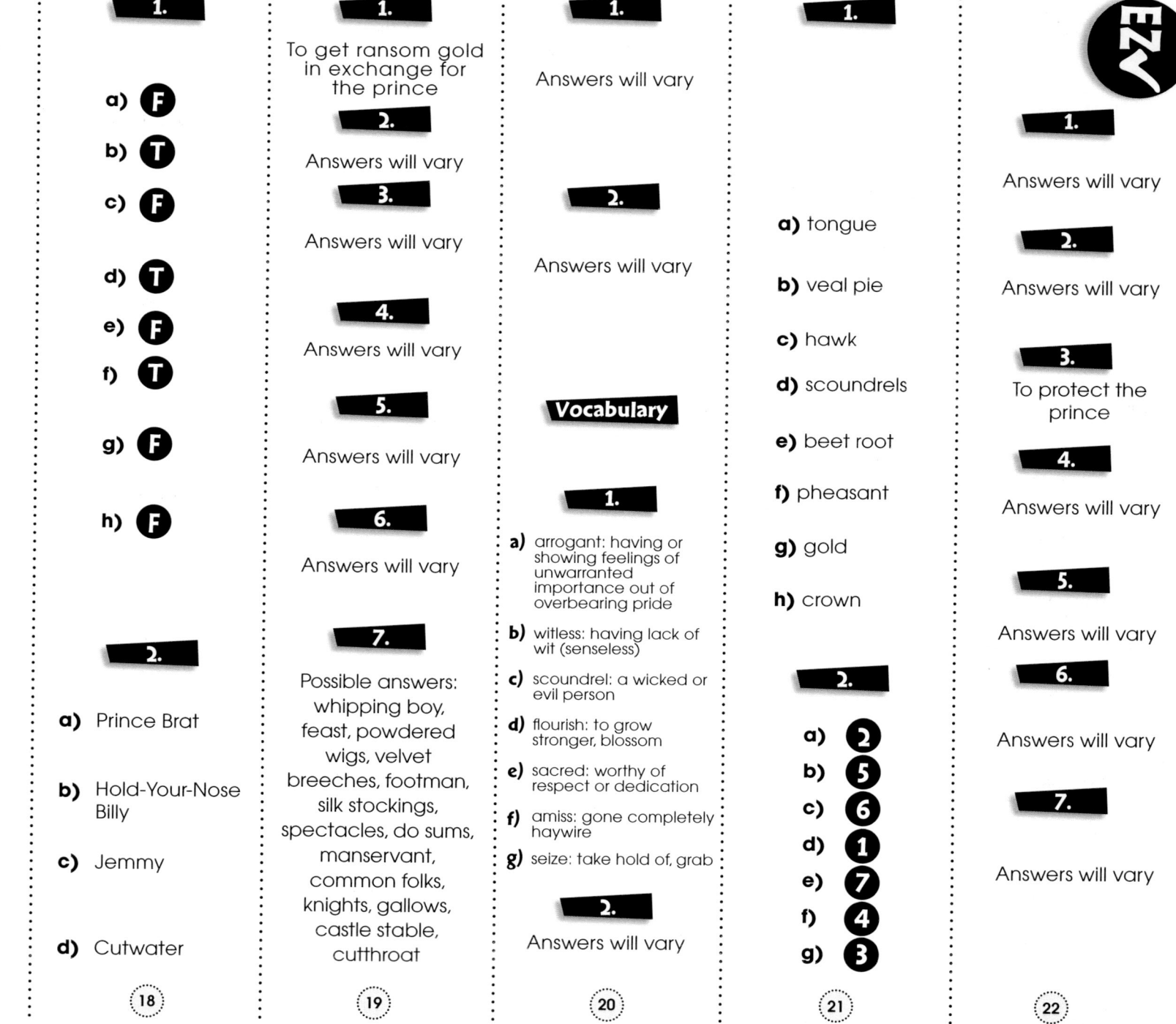

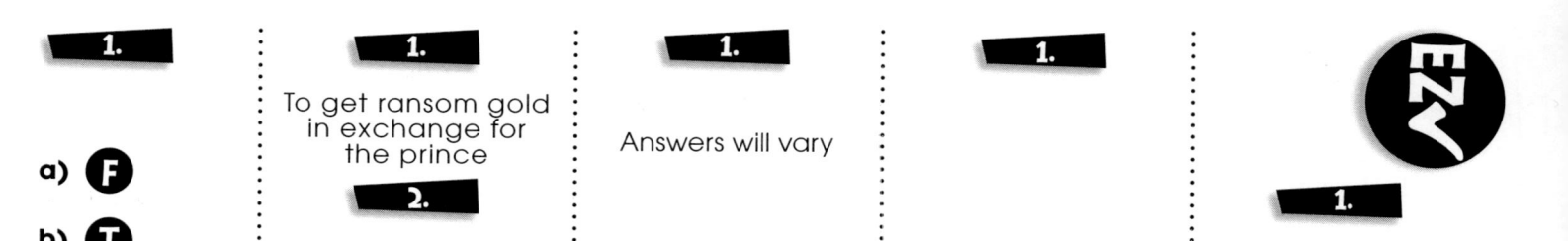

22
1. Answers will vary
2. Answers will vary
3. To protect the prince
4. Answers will vary
5. Answers will vary
6. Answers will vary
7. Answers will vary

21
1.
   a) tongue
   b) veal pie
   c) hawk
   d) scoundrels
   e) beet root
   f) pheasant
   g) gold
   h) crown
2.
   a) 2
   b) 5
   c) 6
   d) 1
   e) 7
   f) 4
   g) 3

20
1. Answers will vary
2. Answers will vary

Vocabulary
1.
   a) arrogant: having or showing feelings of unwarranted importance out of overbearing pride
   b) witless: having lack of wit (senseless)
   c) scoundrel: a wicked or evil person
   d) flourish: to grow stronger, blossom
   e) sacred: worthy of respect or dedication
   f) amiss: gone completely haywire
   g) seize: take hold of, grab
2. Answers will vary

19
1. To get ransom gold in exchange for the prince
2. Answers will vary
3. Answers will vary
4. Answers will vary
5. Answers will vary
6. Answers will vary
7. Possible answers: whipping boy, feast, powdered wigs, velvet breeches, footman, silk stockings, spectacles, do sums, manservant, common folks, knights, gallows, castle stable, cutthroat

---

18
1.
   a) F
   b) T
   c) F
   d) T
   e) F
   f) T
   g) F
   h) F
2.
   a) Prince Brat
   b) Hold-Your-Nose Billy
   c) Jemmy
   d) Cutwater

17
1. Answers will vary
2. Answers will vary

Vocabulary
1. thunderclap
2. awe
3. wisps
4. thatched
5. bleated
6. ruffian
7. rogue
8. exploit

© CLASSROOM COMPLETE PRESS

The Whipping Boy CC2508

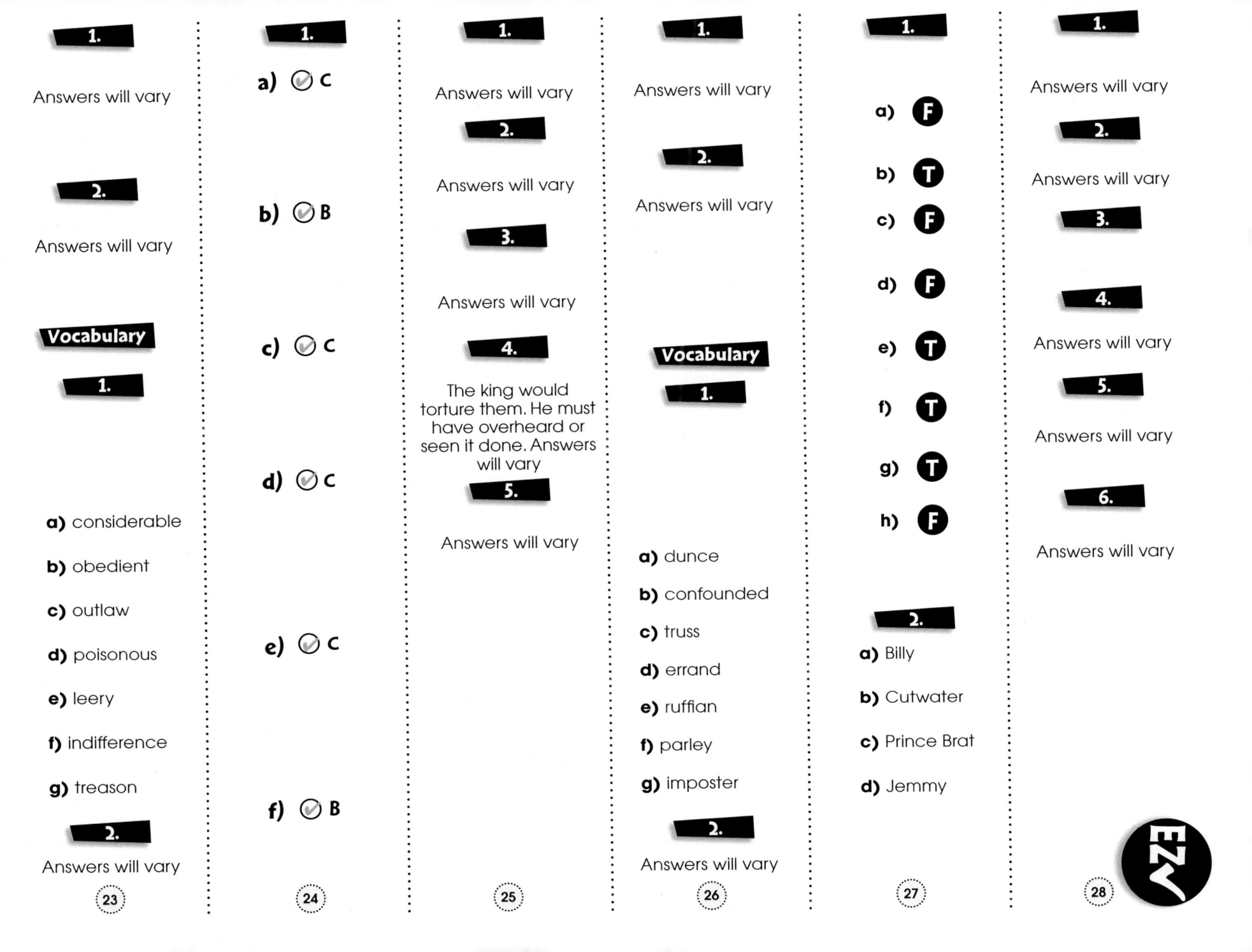

28
1. Answers will vary
2. Answers will vary
3. Answers will vary
4. Answers will vary
5. Answers will vary
6. Answers will vary

27
1.
   a) F
   b) T
   c) F
   d) F
   e) T
   f) T
   g) T
   h) F
2.
   a) Billy
   b) Cutwater
   c) Prince Brat
   d) Jemmy

26
1. Answers will vary
2. Answers will vary

Vocabulary
1.
   a) dunce
   b) confounded
   c) truss
   d) errand
   e) ruffian
   f) parley
   g) imposter
2. Answers will vary

25
1. Answers will vary
2. Answers will vary
3. Answers will vary
4. Answers will vary
5. The king would torture them. He must have overheard or seen it done. Answers will vary
6. Answers will vary

24
1.
   a) C
   b) B
   c) C
   d) C
   e) C
   f) B

23
1. Answers will vary
2. Answers will vary

Vocabulary
1.
   a) considerable
   b) obedient
   c) outlaw
   d) poisonous
   e) leery
   f) indifference
   g) treason
2. Answers will vary

The Whipping Boy CC2508

EZ✓

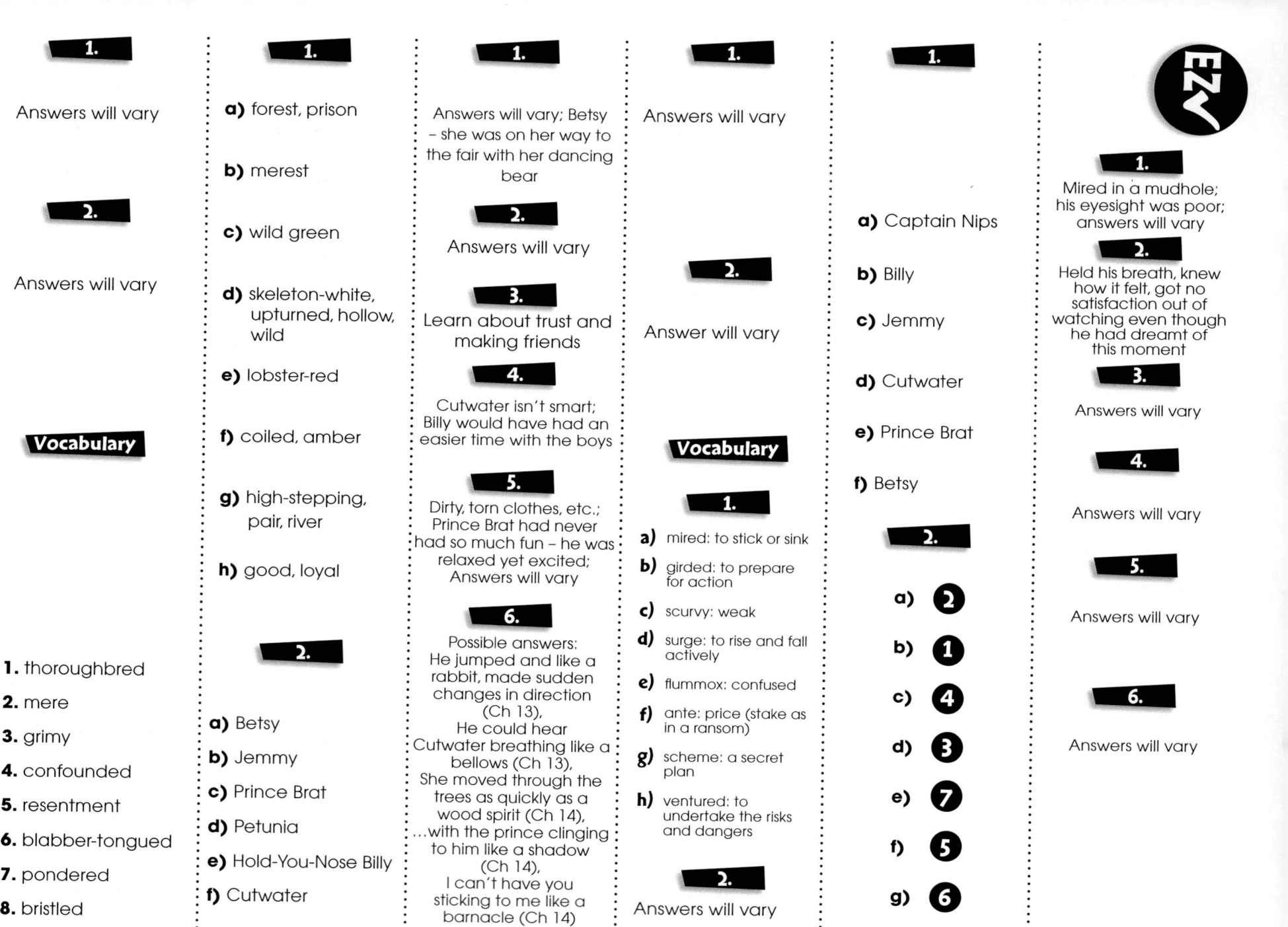

Page 34

1. Mired in a mudhole; his eyesight was poor; answers will vary
2. Held his breath, knew how it felt, got no satisfaction out of watching even though he had dreamt of this moment
3. Answers will vary
4. Answers will vary
5. Answers will vary
6. Answers will vary

Page 33

1.
   a) Captain Nips
   b) Billy
   c) Jemmy
   d) Cutwater
   e) Prince Brat
   f) Betsy

2.
   a) 2
   b) 1
   c) 4
   d) 3
   e) 7
   f) 5
   g) 6

Page 32

1. Answers will vary
2. Answer will vary

Vocabulary

1.
   a) mired: to stick or sink
   b) girded: to prepare for action
   c) scurvy: weak
   d) surge: to rise and fall actively
   e) flummox: confused
   f) ante: price (stake as in a ransom)
   g) scheme: a secret plan
   h) ventured: to undertake the risks and dangers

2. Answers will vary

Page 31

1. Answers will vary; Betsy – she was on her way to the fair with her dancing bear
2. Answers vary
3. Learn about trust and making friends
4. Cutwater isn't smart; Billy would have had an easier time with the boys
5. Dirty, torn clothes, etc.; Prince Brat had never had so much fun – he was relaxed yet excited; Answers will vary
6. Possible answers:
   - He jumped and like a rabbit, made sudden changes in direction (Ch 13),
   - He could hear Cutwater breathing like a bellows (Ch 13),
   - She moved through the trees as quickly as a wood spirit (Ch 14),
   - ...with the prince clinging to him like a shadow (Ch 14),
   - I can't have you sticking to me like a barnacle (Ch 14)

Page 30

1.
   a) forest, prison
   b) merest
   c) wild green
   d) skeleton-white, upturned, hollow, wild
   e) lobster-red
   f) coiled, amber
   g) high-stepping, pair, river
   h) good, loyal

2.
   a) Betsy
   b) Jemmy
   c) Prince Brat
   d) Petunia
   e) Hold-You-Nose Billy
   f) Cutwater

Page 29

1. Answers will vary
2. Answers will vary

Vocabulary

1. thoroughbred
2. mere
3. grimy
4. confounded
5. resentment
6. blabber-tongued
7. pondered
8. bristled

© CLASSROOM COMPLETE PRESS

The Whipping Boy CC2508

EZ ✓

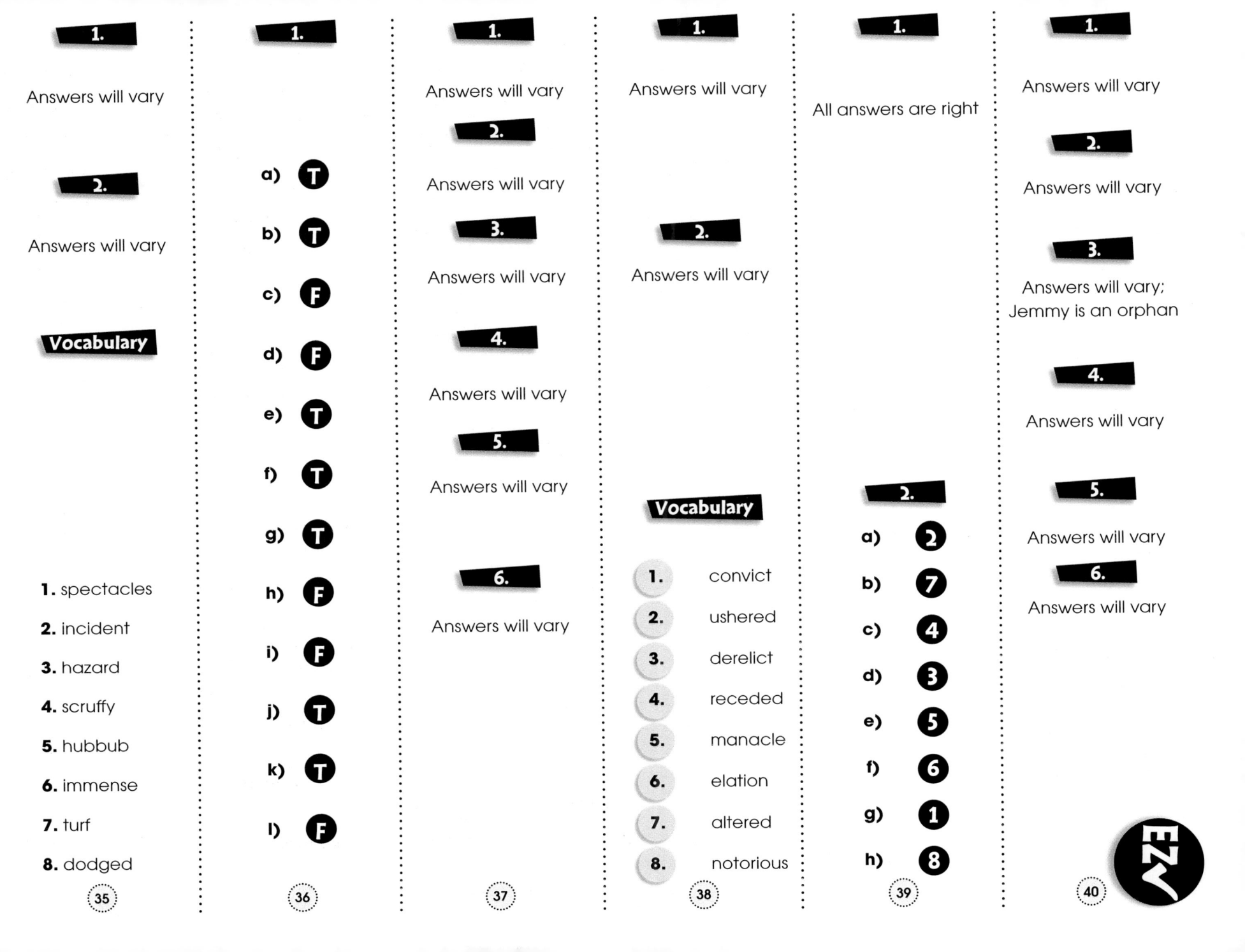

Page 40
1. Answers will vary
2. Answers will vary
3. Answers will vary; Jemmy is an orphan
4. Answers will vary
5. Answers will vary
6. Answers will vary

Page 39
1. All answers are right
2.
   a) 2
   b) 7
   c) 4
   d) 3
   e) 5
   f) 6
   g) 1
   h) 8

Page 38
1. Answers will vary
2. Answers will vary

Vocabulary
1. convict
2. ushered
3. derelict
4. receded
5. manacle
6. elation
7. altered
8. notorious

Page 37
1. Answers will vary
2. Answers will vary
3. Answers will vary
4. Answers will vary
5. Answers will vary
6. Answers will vary

Page 36
1.
   a) T
   b) T
   c) F
   d) F
   e) T
   f) T
   g) T
   h) F
   i) F
   j) T
   k) T
   l) F

Page 35
1. Answers will vary
2. Answers will vary

Vocabulary
1. spectacles
2. incident
3. hazard
4. scruffy
5. hubbub
6. immense
7. turf
8. dodged

Word Search Answers

1. Major: Prince Brat, Jemmy
Minor: Master Peckwit, Hold-Your-Nose Billy, Cutwater, Betsy, Petunia, Captain Nips

2. He is bored; brings Jemmy, the whipping boy, with him because he is afraid of the dark

3. When Smudge meets up with Jemmy, Jemmy realizes that he will miss reading and writing; He realizes how ignorant he was before he was sent to the castle

4. Betsy is a young girl who is taking her dancing bear to the fair; Twice the bear scares off the two outlaws

5. He is mischievous, gets into lots of trouble, and doesn't have to suffer the consequences of his actions; he has his whipping boy, beaten instead

6. Bullied by outlaws; Hold-Your-Nose Billy and Cutwater are thieves and murderers

7. Billy wanted to write a ransom note but only Jemmy could write. The boys switched identities so that Jemmy could protect the real Prince.

8. Twice he gave the boys a ride; full of potatoes (food which he shared with the boys)

9. Betsy' bear; scares off the outlaws twice in a row; Petunia dances and Betsy collects coins for food for the boys

10. Old man in the sewer tunnels; keeps his candle out and tell the outlaws to go in the opposite direction of the two boys

11. Felt terrible even though he had dreamt of this day; told the Prince to bawl

12. Potatoes, and then money for a mug of warm, fresh milk

13. A bear, named Petunia

14. The whipping boy received the punishment the prince should have received but was never given; found living in the streets

15. Meat pies, fruit tarts, brace of roast pheasant, China plate, silver spoon, silver knife. Answers will vary, but more food, blankets, extra clothes are acceptable answers.

16. Handkerchiefs, shoes, ladies' combs, cowbell; looking for some paper

17. Prince Brat asked Betsy to turn in Jemmy; The king forgave the boys

18. In a kingdom in the medieval times

Comparing Characters

Use the Venn diagram to record the character traits that are unique to Prince Brat and Jemmy. Where the ovals overlap, write down the traits that they have in common.

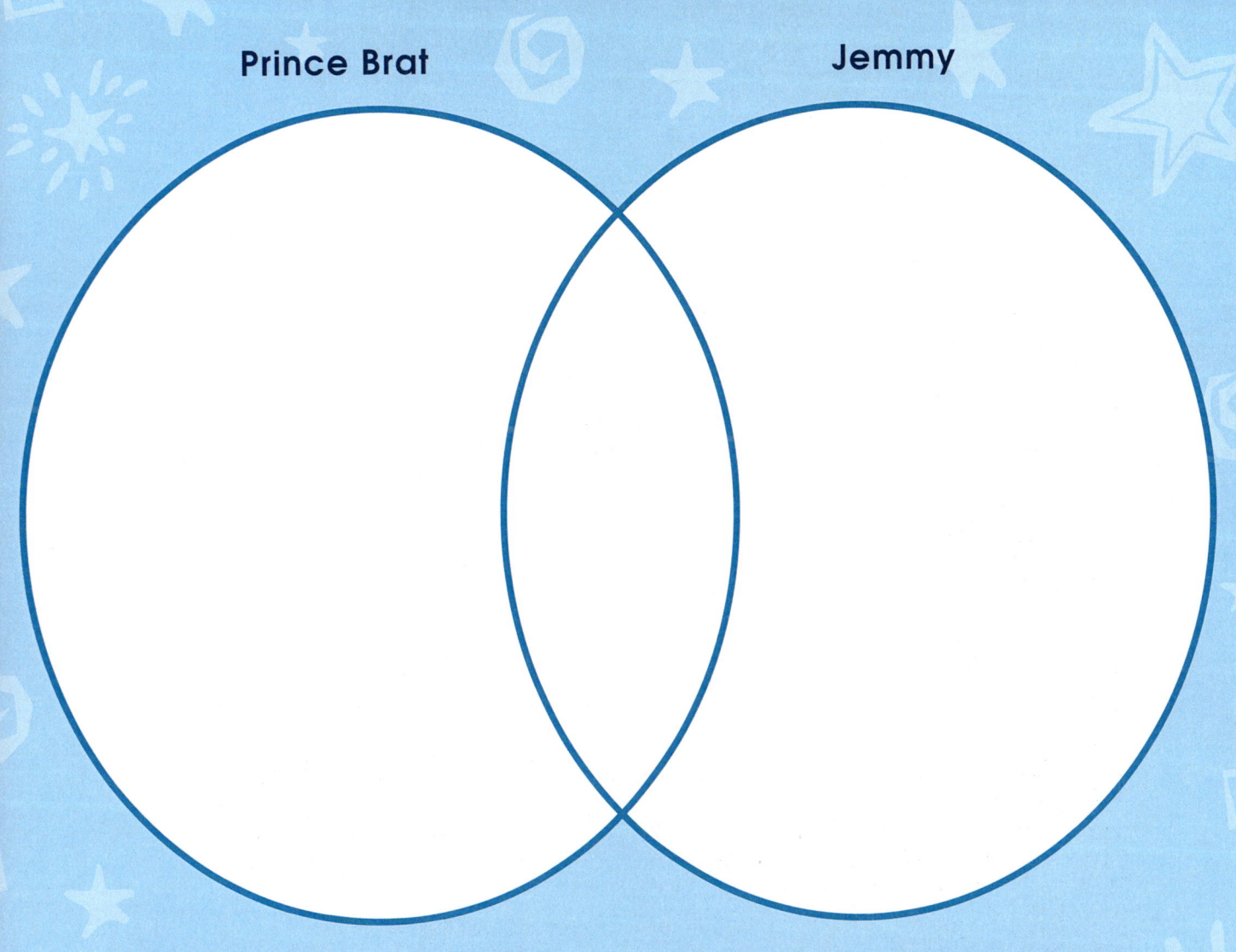

Prince Brat   Jemmy

Which character would you prefer to have as a friend – the Prince or Jemmy? Give three reasons for your answer.

_____
_____
_____

Before and After

In the first column of the chart, describe the kind of person Prince Brat was at the beginning of the novel. In the second column, describe how he had changed by the end of the novel. What kind of person had he become? How had he grown and matured as a person?

1. Prince Brat at the beginning of the novel	2. How had Prince Brat matured by the end of the novel?

Sequencing the Story

Write the main ideas and main events in the novel, The Whipping Boy, in chronological order.

1.
2.
3.
4.
5.
6.
7.
8.
9.
10.